Treble Clef

for the Viola

by Cassia Harvey

CHP223

©2013 by C. Harvey Publications All Rights Reserved.

www.charveypublications.com - print books
www.learnstrings.com - PDF downloadable books
www.harveystringarrangements.com - chamber music

Treble Clef Note Charts

Note Names

Open Strings

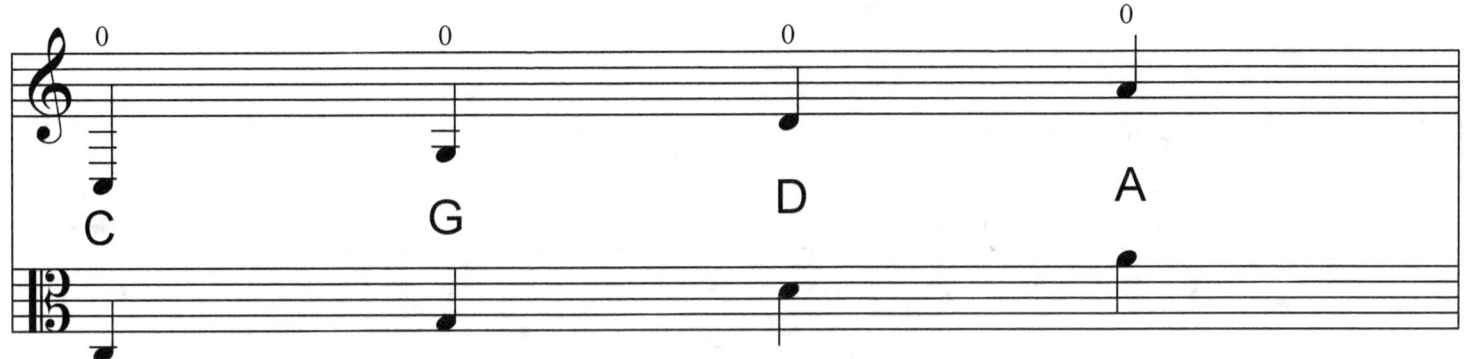

Playing in Treble Clef

The Note "C"

Treble Clef for the Viola

Cassia Harvey

Playing C in a finger exercise:

©2013 C. Harvey Publications All Rights Reserved.

Treble Clef for the Viola

Canon
Tallis

Lord Randal
Trad.

©2013 C. Harvey Publications All Rights Reserved.

The Note "B"

Finger Exercise

Treble Clef for the Viola

The Grey Goose
Trad.

Blow the Man Down
Trad.

©2013 C. Harvey Publications All Rights Reserved.

Treble Clef for the Viola

The Note "D"

The Note "A"

Treble Clef for the Viola

All Through the Night
Trad.

Two Russian Folk Songs
Trad.

©2013 C. Harvey Publications All Rights Reserved.

Treble Clef for the Viola

The Note "E"

Skipping Notes

©2013 C. Harvey Publications All Rights Reserved.

Treble Clef for the Viola

The Jasmine Flower
Trad.

My Homeland
Gretchaninoff

The Note "G"

G through E in treble clef

Treble Clef for the Viola

Theme from Don Giovanni and Variation
Mozart

Czech Folk Dance
Trad.

©2013 C. Harvey Publications All Rights Reserved.

The Note "F"

The Note "F#"

Treble Clef for the Viola
13

Theme from Clarinet Concerto Mozart

Minuet Mozart

©2013 C. Harvey Publications All Rights Reserved.

The Note "G"

Changing Clefs

Treble Clef for the Viola

Slavonic Dance
Dvorak

Mahmina, mihlaja
Trad. Latvian

Now try to read the entire tune in treble clef:

©2013 C. Harvey Publications All Rights Reserved.

Treble Clef for the Viola

The Note "A"

Treble Clef in A Major

Treble Clef for the Viola

Folk Song
Trad. Latvian

March
Bast

©2013 C. Harvey Publications All Rights Reserved.

The Note "B"

The Note "B♭"

Treble Clef for the Viola

My Ain Kind Dearie-O — Trad. Scottish

Air — Anon.

©2013 C. Harvey Publications All Rights Reserved.

Treble Clef for the Viola

The Note "C"

The Note "C#"

Treble Clef for the Viola

The Note "D"

Skipping Notes

Treble Clef for the Viola

Aria
Handel

Treble Clef for the Viola

Dance Neapolitan
Tchaikovsky

Treble Clef for the Viola

Sharps and Flats

Arpeggios

Treble Clef for the Viola
Moto Perpetuo
Paganini

©2013 C. Harvey Publications All Rights Reserved.

The Note "F#"

Treble Clef and Third Position

Treble Clef for the Viola

Third Position Study No. 1
Harvey

Scheherazade
Rimsky-Korsakov

©2013 C. Harvey Publications All Rights Reserved.

Treble Clef for the Viola

The Note "G"

Across Strings

Treble Clef for the Viola

Third Position Study No. 2

The Two Ravens
Trad., arr. Harvey

Treble Clef for the Viola

Scales in Third Position

Arpeggios in Third Position

Treble Clef for the Viola

Minuet
Bach

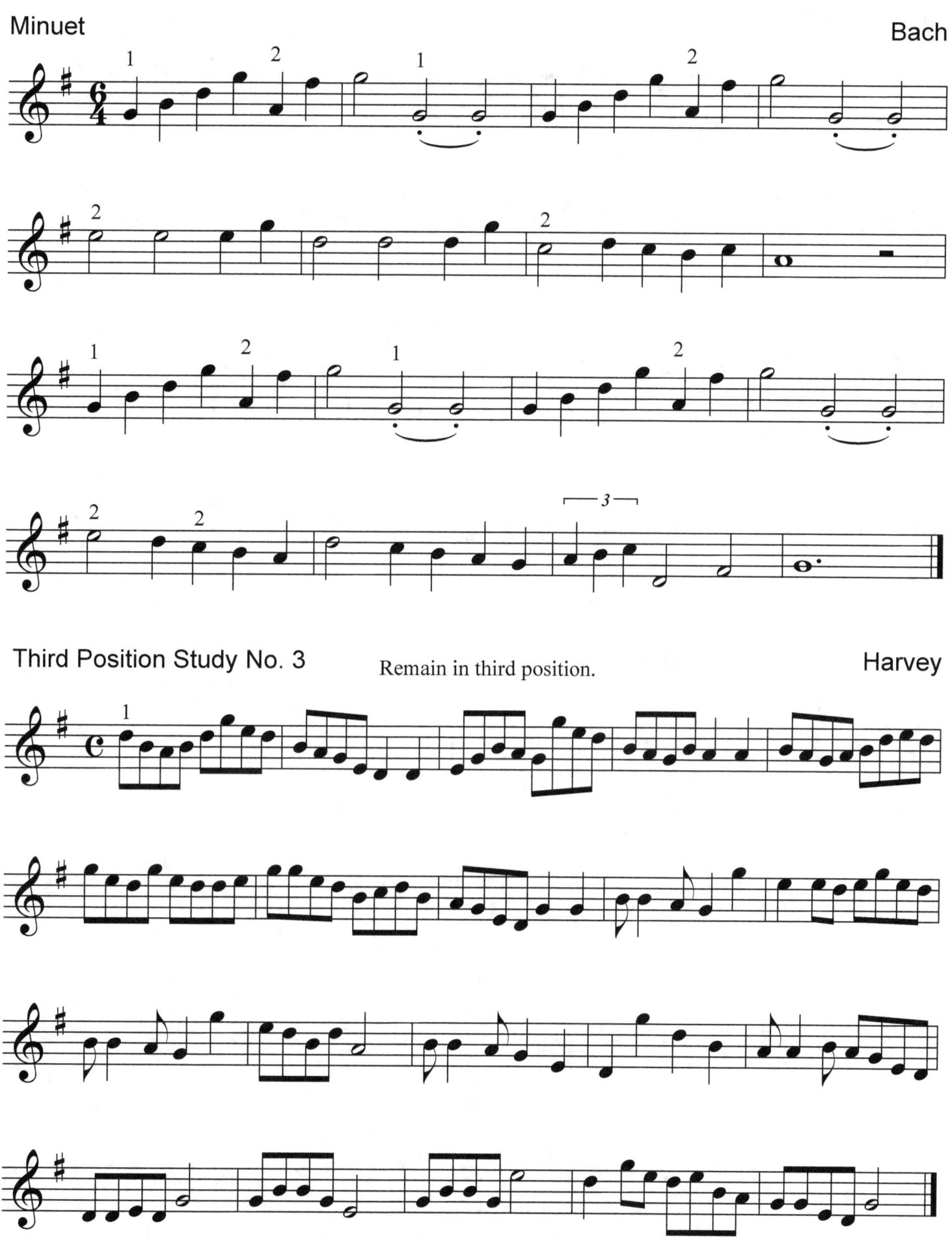

Third Position Study No. 3
Remain in third position.
Harvey

©2013 C. Harvey Publications All Rights Reserved.

Treble Clef for the Viola

Ribbon Dance
Trad. English, arr. Harvey

Fifth Position Fiddle Tune

Remain in fifth position for the rest of the piece.

©2013 C. Harvey Publications All Rights Reserved.

F Major Treble Clef Study

Gavotte
Telemann, arr. Harvey

Treble Clef for the Viola

B♭ Major Treble Clef Study

Musette
Cais D'Hervelois, arr. Harvey

©2013 C. Harvey Publications All Rights Reserved.

Treble Clef for the Viola

39

F major scale

G major scale

A♭ major scale

A major scale

B♭ major scale

©2013 C. Harvey Publications All Rights Reserved.

Also available from www.charveypublications.com: CHP353 Open String Bow Workouts for Viola, Book One

This book of new and exciting bowing workouts for the viola gives you 97 exercises to train your bow on open strings before you begin the rest of your practice.

Since there are no left hand notes, you can focus entirely on improving the dexterity and control of the right (bow) hand.

Useful also for students who are struggling with reading notes, this book gives violists a tremendous resource for creating better tone.

The exercises work on on bow distribution, rests and retaking bows, slurs, triplets, dotted rhythms, double stops, string crossing and more.

www.ingramcontent.com/pod-product-compliance
Lightning Source LLC
Chambersburg PA
CBHW051427070526
44584CB00023B/3609